E

L

Metamorphosis

Written and edited by
Erik & Emily
Langford

Index

10 introduction micro
11 what is enough
12 insomnia dreamweaver
13 untitled
14- continiued
15 micro
16 roots and wings
17 quote
18 mountains and molehills
19 blackberry bruises
20 continued
21 and now there ios us
23 my girl
24 i choose my darkness
25 continued
26 the spider and the passionflower
27 snow day
28 untitled

29 no one
30 continued
31 rebirth
32 quote
33 lucid sunshine rain
34 folded soul
36 the apples grow red in the graveyard
37 micro
38 six degrees
39 Sunday
40 untitled
41 micro
42 she has a heart that was made to love
43 micro
44 Yew
45 thoughts 14/09/2022
46 micro

48 with the softest smile

49 lifeless woodland

50 closet freak

51 quote

52 September's clutch

53 lay me to rest

54 does your ribcage bloom too?

55 then and now

56 eight years of healing

57 continued

58 quote

60 untitled

61 i love you seven

62 clothesline

63 quote

64 psalm 1

65-67 the church of us

48 with the softest smile
49 lifeless woodland
50 closet freak
51 quote
52 September's clutch
53 lay me to rest
54 does your ribcage bloom too?
55 then and now
56 eight years of healing
57 continued
58 quote
60 untitled
61 i love you seven
62 clothesline
63 quote
64 psalm 1
65-67 the church of us

70 the veil
71 you, them and i
72 micro
74 old oak
75 quote
76 untitled
77 the tenth month
78 yet another death
79 continued
80 dare to live
81 surrendering
82 ive tried
83 quote
84 micro
86 quote
87 micro
88 untitled
89 affirmation
90 body and all

91 body and all
92 micro
93 no rainbows and butterflies
94 quote
95 micro
96 six degrees
98 untitled
100 micro
101 quote
102 the wolf and the willow
103 collapsed
104 hellfire
105 quote
106 quote
107 snow falls
108 untitled
109 quote
110 my hands
112 church of us

116 idols
117 the trees are about to show you
118 micro
119 chronic pain
120 beautifully rambuntious
121 micro
122 micro
124 equinoc and the horse chestnut tree
125

Poetry

We are taught so intrinsically
that life is about finding certainty,
when in actuality it is about being okay
with how uncertain everything is.

What is enough?

I often wonder if I pray enough?
give thanks enough for living.

If there were a number to such things
I would definitely not meet it,
I can be caught dwindling, hopping
the laced shadows of the trees,
or swimming between the pages of prose-
running my fingers across the spines birthed
by minds not unlike mine.

does prayer look like finding new birds to
mark off in a bird finder book?
does giving thanks look like picking berries from
wild bushes and serving them to friends with tea?

I often wonder if i pray enough,
I forget to stop,
I am living the life I'm given.

Insomnia dreamweaver

I can't sleep
my mind is a restless mortuary
of endless deaths.

smoke screens of a life yet to be loved,
hang in macrame garlands in unreachable gardens.

I can't sleep.
        It's a disease of sorts.

tangible moments shatter at my touch. bleeding into
corners of a vision I'm not sure I've ever seen.

I can't sleep.
        but I continue to dream

i wear half my heart on my sleeve
it's so cliché, what isn't these days
the other half is around my neck
and a third half, that doesn't make sense,
a third half is stuck to a space heater beside my bed
half my heart, and the whole fucking Sun
pardon my language
i don't know what comes over me sometimes
sometimes i say "fuck" just because
i like the way it feels on my tongue
and for the same reason, you
it excites me, i'm an excitable person
skittish even, impish most definitely
i know every lover by name
but can only name one who loves me for me
the rest stay tucked in the cupboard
i place her on the window sill
with the goat skull, bits of bark, stones
and other shiny magicians
if you're a believer in moon magic, anyway
she and they soak in its light every four weeks
and for the same reason, i sit outside at night.

this is all completely normal to me
i ramble on in here like a lunatic because it's
 "once in a while" i fall in love
and only once i've felt truly safe
and that's a hell of a streak
for someone who runs a lot
who has a heart in at least three places,
to the best of my knowledge
and thats a hell of a lot of choice/work/luck
to find love that can watch you move a mile a minute
and still say it's a home you've got,
despite the madness
the mayhem
the melancholy
the mmm...what's the word for it?
mental problems, man.

how I'd cling to your cold metal
how I'd hold you, when mourning winter
brings its bitter air

Roots and wings

you can adorn roots and wings,
this is something I have learnt recently.
I take note from my love of the trees
and dreams of having freedom
akin to the birds

but today I wander, featherless,
without soils to bury myself in.

I know of their existence,
for i feel there absence
I feel the loss

"I love you so much, but please can you not touch me today"

Mountains and molehills

pluck me from this madness
and press me between the
pages of your flesh
as I climb these
mountains carved
   from molehills

for I tire-
 of the   wax   and   wane
of my own mind
      trying to survive
when I lose myself in fervour

such contradictions
 in the forest of my own head
little meadows of
     fractured sunlight
appear in the thickets of endless death

so will you?
     pluck me from this madness
and press me between the
pages of your flesh

Blackberry bruises

I plucked blackberries in October,
little purple fists roll around nervously
atop a platter of flesh
    same as before only aged

to taste such sweetness
paired with a time my pallet
should lie sour
pulls something from me

I am held here. there-
  In a space of nothingness
    b r i m m i n g
with everything all at once

    unsatisfied

falling endlessly into autumns arms
having never felt so uncertain
I've become nervous of the burden-
  I place upon myself

a bruise shade of unsullied innocence
rolls itself between her fingers
   then my own

 briar snags the insides of a voiceless
throat as my song resides in the hollows
   of a blackbirds belly
stolen from the very bush
    I forage from each October

- and now there is us -

every evening, i find myself in a dream
lapping at the rivers laughter, i drink every drop
soak my eyes to capacity in your sunshine yellow hello
and wash my skin of muddy worries with wonder
the pen puffs popcorn clouds
my pillow talks to me as i read aloud
we wept at the poets departure, you remember
the Love that was there
after the eternal fire and the steep stairs
and the sleep on the bedrock
where we awoke with one another.
you came back, you always do, from somewhere out there
in the mirror, most likely
she makes a flower crown, and is quite content
with copper and uncut gems.
i couldn't help but smirk just now
at the thought of you thinking
you're too much or, ironically, not enough.
i manifested you on a midnight stroll
with the milk of the moon
i poured a bowl to the brim of self reflection
and when i made it to the last spoonful, i fell in
Love with myself,   and then there was you.

my girl goes somewhere else sometimes
feels the need to apologise but I don't mind
i lay her on her side and kiss her goodnight
tell her I wanna be beside her for the rest of my life
times of light or times of strife,
it doesn't matter I'll wipe her tears and
fill her chest with laughter
listen to her fears and thoughts on what comes after
come what may that's what I say
and we're same same but different
I'm a stray dog and she's a tree top, glistenin'
a sunny ray on a rainy day and a grey cloud on an
otherwise clear blue day
the perfectly imperfect rendition of yin and yang
but we still take time to talk and dedicate
never give up and uncomplicate

Today I chose to hide in my darkness

I have run out of air, lungs failing me and I can't quite
 tell if I want to fight.   (I'm exhausted)
   Or if I surrender maybe I'll be happy…..

Today I chained myself to a bed in the dark because the alternative is,
  the light will expose all that is me.

failing at living is my specialty apparently-
   rationality burns through me screaming it's all the meds,
     (scrolls of side effects almost all read)

"May cause depressive or suicidal thoughts"

 but hey they are keeping me alive so there's -

Some light, right?

but thoughts, they creep in
 tentacles tickle at my dopamine and it feels good to see a way out,
open a door and there it is ….. the escape from the darkness,
the sunshine, the way out.

temptations' vibrations run its course through my
 battered veins and I rattle myself deeper into the darkness
adding extra chains to the bed.

   it's a day
   it's just the meds
   It's just a day

the spider and the passion flower

webbed intricacy lies dormant in the underbelly
of my pen, i use its darkness as my ally,
stolen virtuosity hangs spun between the silken teardrops
of lies I hum to myself.

ten fingers meet in the centre of the earth wrapped in the
thorns of its past, in the blooms of the present,
in the season of its fall.

A twisted cornucopia of thoughts are yet to come to pass,
but it lies there still, yet open in the space where I am whole.

Snowday

she was now just one, yet done,
of the two suns left to fade in the orbit of his
Love.
the sky opened itself up today
I think i'll fall with the snow

gently
slowly
on purpose

no one has ever loved me like you
no one has ever said to me
you're broken and it's beautiful
and sat with me in the glass
you left the glue and ulterior motives at home
wherever home was way back when
when we got away with nonsense
you call me out on myself
hold me close when you hold me accountable
somehow stern and gentle
you make me, no, you help me become
something different, I won't say better,
but more myself
feel free to explore myself
there's always been a part of me that is
over-emotional, under-approachable
hilariously hysterical, undoubtedly irritable
you have called me complex before
you're not the first
not of this world
the fifth planet in possibility, love, and stature
you are the first to simplify my being
you don't take credit for that
I call you humble, you call me silly
we get things backwards and talk to ourselves

we laugh it all off
I'll say it again and again until you get it
no one has ever loved me like you
I feel like I've been seen before,
but I was only Loved in bits and pieces
I wake up every morning knowing your Love in whole

Rebirth

the wind plays its melodies
with the bones of winters graveyards,
a song of mourning permeates,
my bedroom window,   spooling. in. grief

i feel their lost hope
i see it in the flourishing in my own
a sunlight swallowed by the throat of a God,
	resurrection flows itself softly, into the rivers of me.

"you are ridiculous"

Lucid sunshine rain

I walk in, to a sad song and the sound of drilling.
you see my face and   b r e a k.
((heavens gates disrupting a bruised skyline))
shoulder shrugging,
lucid, sunshine and rain is all I can
explain, as to what I saw.

you are beautiful when you burst right open,
a chrysalis of emotions;
of unrestrained love.

((All ruptured dam given forest to run and run))

I burst right with you,
a mixture of concern
and pure devotion.

because you,
all lucid sunshine,
reign in the storm of all you are
and
all you will ever become.

Folded soul

time splices my memories
and i am held between the
folds of a blemished soul
a beauteous spirit.   tightly.
spinning an origami tale.   a promise to
never let me.   go

the apples grow red in the graveyard

we wandered through
a maze of falling stones
long left to the elements
the smell of red cedar soaks the wind
silence coats the back of the throat
mementos sit placed beside the long untouched
Mother Earth reclaims her space
roots protrude, pushing and pulling
scattered around its trunk
rotten fruit, a few in perfect form
plucking it from her bosom, we bit into the flesh
crimson crisp seeping under the tongue
and in the cheek
a gift from death has never tasted so sweet

Where are those unconditional lovers
Who truly need nothing for what they give?
is anything done for the sole purpose of charity anymore?

the cool caress
of September's breath
held me this morn'
as I reached into
    gossamer lungs to
        find my own

a shudder crawled itself
under blankets of skin
braiding majesty into my bones

I was summoned to life
moulded by the fingers
of my flourishing

((whispers of a freshening
        borne of bygone sorrow))

today,
I rise under the guise of Autumn
    under eyes half closed
perched upon the corners
    of a smile unpretended9
formed in the belly of a Summer
truly lived
truly loved
truly felt

Sunday will be our day.
we will spend it in soft, little churches,
a prayer said in each step.
we will twirl sermons
and pour testament into two cups.
soon after, we can return to the sun
creeping in to tell secrets to our skin.
for a time, there will be silence
but the quiet will be bath water;
a steeped temple of faith
in our Love.
in the evenings, we might make pilgrimage
into a forest where we can find our friends
and we will pray for us.
we will pray for them.

I couldn't tell the rain from the pain
the flashing headlights from your eyes
I hate to see you crying
I hate to see you falling but I can barely stand on my own
stone walls are all we have to lean on for the time being
I want to be that for you
the words repeat in my head like laying bricks
brick, speaking it into the mortar, brick
I can be more than cold wind
more than torrent jumping from the treetops
soaking skin to bone, it takes time to warm you know
all evening all morning all of times time left
I want to be that for you
let me die trying, darling

Have patience with me please
as I learn again how to be gentle
I've lost a lot this year
and I am so cold

she has a heart that was made to love
to live in
I see the way she sleeps
she smiles
she treats people and places and things
she presses her hands against a tree
her face against me
it all has this dream-like quality
since I said "just be with me already"
and you crossed a planet
in what seemed like an instant
you were in my arms
and all the cut out
carved down
scribed out pieces
had finality

the things you put into the world really
do make there way back to you.

the love I found for my downfalls
and the future I strive to flourish in
looks me in the eyes each morning
we move worlds with one another
we shift separately,
but gravity has us so desperately bound.

the end of the world
Is merely a scratch upon the surface
of unknown truth

Yew

Clouds burst rainfall across my breast
eliciting clarity in vision
    (birthing a endless breath)
 I have become grounded though not
without great loss
    a casualty of one's own undoing

drapes close on former sorrow
      (yet open upon a new death)
a raven beats it wings
gifting flight to the fallen
   a someone left behind
  she summoned Sol from his cradle/ life from the wood
till a newness becomes of its bareness
so soft
so young
        still wandering

Thoughts 14/09/2022

and I wonder if the finality of mortality is
doleful if you are alone in this world?
((would this grief dissipate if
no one were around to feel it?))

You help me revisit places I always knew existed but could never truly embrace, and grow there wildly in love.

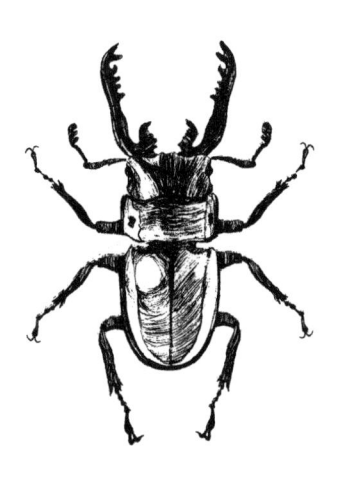

With the softest smile he wiped the pain away

I fell in love once more last night
With fingers teasing suds from matted locks
Untying each knot as if my hair were spun from gold.
My chin rested on your chest.   Eyes locked with the softest
smile I think I've ever seen and I cried at the pitiful spectacle

I hide my swollen body shame rolls itself around my tummy
anchors of embarrassment and disgust claw at whatI see

What I know he sees.

In the silence of this different type of love making he
broke my arms crossing my body, then the silence with

"Don't, please don't ever hide from me"

lifeless woodland

I have found myself
unclothed
in a branchless forest I once knew as home
brambles shackle me into submissive demands plotting
my own demise
I fumble for forgiveness
yet allow shame to roll around my tongue into
weighted cheeks.
if I dont bury myself now-
Into the soils daring to decay beneath my feet
what would be left of this woodland,
under these storms of anguish

will become undone

Closet freak

I like pretty things
like flowers, fields, leaves,
love and light, and at night
I choke them
because they ask
so nicely.

"if you look up the word petty in the dictionary, you would see a picture of your face"

September's clutch

I am afraid of months like these now
days filled with a vibrancy that makes decay delicious
harvesting memories is a slow go this year
A lot like my physical ability to harvest
our mothers seasonal fruits.
(Foraging, rituals and Simmer pots)

Instead something else haunts
 (I am barely of personage nowadays)
Nergals clenched fist has buried
itself between my shoulder blades
cracking its knuckles if i dare to fall asleep

and then , there is September.
 that Month of my birth, my chance to feel alive as a
foreboding breathes thick in a stagnant air
and has stolen the sparklers from this lover's eyes.

Lay me to rest on the mountains and hills

cover my body in pine needles
gathered from the canyon I fell in love
climb to the tree, lonely at the top
of the hill, and say my name into the
wind, one last time. my love for my
country was born here, it should
be only fitting, I should say so myself.
it's should be the place
 where my name should die.

Does your ribcage bloom too?
as our fingers intertwine,
for what feels like the last time;
because it could be, you know?
my mind starts to wander, and so
do your hands, a welcome
distraction to what's happening in
this memory lagoon;
it's a swamp in here, no crystal waters
but what run in ravines down
these cheeks.
      (caught by your lips)

heavy desperate breaths wane
into sighs as we fall deeper
      (deeper still)
and the ideation quiets down,
so i ask, so politely, will you hold
me till its all over;
this hour
this night
this life?
    because right now, despite it all
   in this moment
i bloom for you

Then and now

I walk out into an opening
pools of speckled moonlight pass through
the beechwood canopies yet my feet only
move amongst the shadows

I reach for each puddle with sick desperation
to no avail
 to no avail

I hear everything happening around me
slowly beginning to fade
dreams reality carried away
In a shrouded breath

I look forward to deliberately pass into
the next puddle of blackened uncertainty
fill my lungs with a newness of the only living
moment i have. then let go

that was then. this is now

eight years of healing un-buried by one phone call

Pain is a tangible thing.
an iron fist welting bones and flesh.
making home, weighing itself down in the space
I was deemed a woman.
 a stolen cradle.
a vacuum of disfigured ruins,
haunted by the whispering wails
 of tiny little ghosts wandering in possibility.

and I knew. know.

all these years of relishing in the remarkable
blooms of my innermost sanctuary.

I know.
my feminine stolen on an operating table.
four times nine months of secrets before they
were shared with others
 lost
 for(n)ever

a scrapbook of tissue and blood,
a pantomime of a memories to be flipped through
 for(n)ever futures
 for(n)ever always
THIS Pain is a tangible thing.
a tactile, sour, rotting thing
 it is the final thing to call me mother

a child I never dreamt of having

"could you chew any fucking louder?"

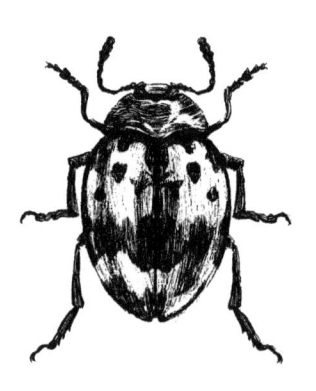

your words reach me just in time
A carrier pigeon with a message on its leg
and all it says is "je t'aime"
the paper smells of you
of what i imagine
of lavender. of the sea.
of something sweet i cant quite put my finger on
(i will save it for when we meet
in the theater of dreams
at the back
seat thirty three B and C
because i see you
and we can just be)
the scenes you paint in your sleep
give the butterflies you describe
it's all we want: a space to read/be read/be read to
kisses in unknown well known places too
the thought of such stamps a single drop
of liquid sunlight on the page, your signature,
and you should know it sparkles there
glistens like the morning sun
rising to make a day
a good day
And it all begins with you.

i love you seven
journaling in hospital

I can't help but hold on to this goodbye from the
lady in the cubicle next to me.
She's old and clearly very unwell, but makes sure she
knows that whoever is on the other end has eaten right.
Needing details of what they ate and drank for the day.
    I love you seven. Call ends.

The power in those few words thread themselves into
my every being.
        Such love. Such a long time.

My mind begins to wonder.... Seven what? Seven days? lives?
Times till they reunite?
Does she know secrets now held upon stars only
she and this person have seen? maybe seven of them.

I will never know because she moved before i did
.... But Wendy, I grew to love you seven too.

you turn my heart
into a hundred yards of clothesline;
as far as the eye can see.
white sheets swaying
in a summer wind.

i close my eyes and see a stretch of green fields
rolling hills, lavender, bluebells
and you-
basket by your side, smiling,
Pulling me in

*"where is ther peanut butter?, -
its right in front of you!"*

Psalm 1
"He is like a tree planted by streams of water"

I sing these words, to a melody of my own tongue,
a tune born in the throat of praise,
adding verses of my own - praising fruits of my own womb,

my kin
the ones that became angels
the ones whose feet have felt the soils of the earth

names when sung they sound as though lullabies
are being sewn into September's wind.

as I nourish my soul in the heavenly streams,
I wash my fruits in prayer, kiss them in promise.

Its there i am feel most holy

I sing
I write
I wash
I promise

we could have this recurring dream, you know?
where two souls can love eachother boundlessly,
and it does not mean they need each other.
a waking lucidity where two hearts beat as one
but nothing expected.

a friendship unlike any other; won't you be there for me?
and it means next to nothing and near everything?
a pace where the advice you give is returned,
and the return you get is self taught.

a connection that confuses the invading eye....
won't you tell them " we talk " ?
that we love eachother like crazy?
that here we are seen and you saved me?
maybe?

there is a place i see you each night in my sleep
the place where two hearts that belong to each other can meet,
comfortable silence is the language we speak.

" can you hear me "? those sighs that are born in our eyes,
breathe life into what's born in our chests.

ground yourself; paddle in puddles
of belonging (finally)
soak yourself in the space now dubbed 'home';
outside of their boxes and labels.

do you think they know of our magic?
of how you gifted me your sight in return for mine?

no desire for questions or confusion;
answers dream outside of lines or limitations.
cut open circumstances like a chrysalis
and hand flight to all that stands in our way.

we never needed them to understand.
we have never, and will never, require them
to see this for what it is; friendship in the mirror.

'friendship' a word so simple yet weaved into constellations
of complexity when cast upon a layman's gaze.
this is the gift of familiarity dressed in the coat of new fabric,
It's always there just waiting to be worn.

Will you be my friend forever?
In this life before this, and the next?
From the dawn of time until it sets?

yes

The Veil

Octobers days fall like the sycamore
leaves outside of my window,
the trees, a wilderness thinning with the veil.

I open myself up with a prayer,
one that summons more than.
more than here
more than now
open to all that was lost.

Samhain i will reach upon the 31st day,
beyond the veil, holding the taken.
soft whispers are now heard outside
of our dreams. No longer concealed
there   while we   here

night has stolen day from the skies pockets
sewing her darkness back in its place.
and we, the ones born in the dark,
ones who find solace in the night dance
between worlds. In hope and in promise.
we reach the other side.

You, them and i

we grew together,
then grew them together, you and i.
we danced till the sun would rise,
then fall with it later that day.
time spent apart never changed hearts .

we grew together
then grew them together
now they have grown and you cry.
we cry together.
we've cried together for years, you and i.

they will keep growing,
as we will together,
time will keep ticking,
as will our hearts
for each other,
you, them and i

a profesion of love
i
am
still
breathing

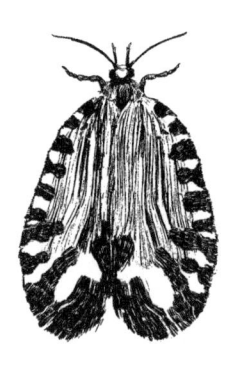

I'm sitting beneath the old oak
I see the footpaths, the memories
hear the chatter, the laughter
a shadow silhouette of what used to be
of what has come to pass
at long last, I can't help but see the ghost of myself
of you
everywhere we've been
remnants in time sifting through the undergrowth
of love and pain
I wonder how many times my toes might touch
one place, one after the other
is the dirt all the same? Impartial
to our presence but by the Gods,
do I see it now
an imprint on the chambers of a compassionate heart
the same as yours
beating, breathing
alive and captured
in light.
in time.

"Its too hot for a bed this small, I'm sleeping on the sofa"

...and it was picturesque
an impromptu living room slow dance
cold and broken before victory
you know the words.

it was blurry before the diamonds
a shoulder blade cuts glass
I was holding you like it was the last time
because it nearly was, and we were afraid

and something saved
you.

the tenth month

I lost myself in the tenth month
pieces of me discarded with the
strings of guts from gourds.

fabricated smiles hang in the darkness:
a moon's sickle forced sideways for love.
a thing strayed for good. gone.

what was given? a stranger.
as times needles thread, barely,
yet heavy upon the surface of
a newness i am forced to follow.

Yet another death

In the end
make love to me in my shadows
hold my silhouette close as i harness my
beautiful darkness,
my violent undoing
Dylan Thomas said
"rage rage against the dying of the light"
and I felt that.
I needed to feel that.
 become the sun
 become the end,
 a broken Earth held In the palms of a broken God.

 stand here in my storms-
I S C R E A M I am angry
the names, the pains, the losses, the grief,
the fucking never ending grief.
though in the end
I'll be found in my burning light casting
shadows of who I am, who I was unaloud to be.

i am the sun.
i am the end

So please i ask In whispered tones, and gritted teeth politely,
hold me with desire, in my desire to unapologetically
break myself in half to set myself free.

This year I dare myself to live / to actually thrive myself alive in the presence of my up and coming / allow the violence of my mind to settle / for it to be born into the dawn of a new day / i will catch sunsets and rises in the tears pulled from eyes, no longer cruel / but truthful / seeing beauty in a body that saved my life / count the scars as stars in search for a place to rest, be blessed they chose me as their night sky / wear griefs crimson coat with a little more strength/ a little more grace / find purpose in the mundane / search for stillness in the chaos of a world determined to watch itself burn / this year i dare myself to live / this year i start again, again

Surrendering

I can feel the rolling hills calling
waves of emerald green leaning into
windy swept days.
 leaning into me.
I can all but surrender to her summons..

maybe somewhere i'll discover the little lost pieces
of who i used to be
•

I have tried to show my love in ways other than words
like the certainty of your eating and drinking
and a good night's sleep.
I love to clean for you. I love to cook for you.
I love to care for you.
I find odd beauty in the way you hang wet laundry,
and the pride you take in the scent of bleach.
I've never seen a bed made more pristine,
a silly hat worn so confidently,
or a sultry jest performed so hilariously.
I still wish I could climb inside and show you what I see
 because the words fall short now don't they?
the actions have become so loud. Like sirens.
like the drunks in the alley.
Like the scent of Marijuana
 outside our door.
I want to show you the fireworks again,
explosively unexpected
because you're as beautiful as they are, my love,
an electric night. The wind on the autumn oak.
The park bench at night, you never were not.

"its like talking to a brick wall"

Do you not see?
The light, it was never really there....

It was merely the moon falling into her own eclipse;
 night's shackles bled melancholy into the very air she breathed until she became it.

" it just feel like we are going round in circles here "

we are not who we were
so give us time to grieve, and
give us time to love again

I hold a feather, it mirrors itself
it's the softest I've ever felt
pressed between hundreds of pages
we were strangers once
now I lather soap where you can't reach
rub your feet while you are weak
the water is hot. I adjust it
accidentally spraying you in the face
exclaim "I didn't mean to!" and do it again
we laugh, you cry
because I'm here for you..?
resting your hands on my shoulders
your head on my chest
I run my hands through your hair
scrubbing, shampooing, rinsing, conditioning
taking care to untangle, treat, and
not tug too hard
taking care of you, it mirrors itself
it's the softest I've ever felt

Affirmation

I choose to wake up and breathe each day,
therefore I am my greatest gift.

My soul is as old as the Rockies,
my eyes as new as a freshly fallen sky,

My existence is undiluted poetry
Who needs a pen to be a poet

Body and all

I think about leaving sometimes.
taking nothing but the clothes on my back and a ruck
sack full of snacks. I would just disappear to anywhere
Other than here, I'd walk until the soles of
my chucks wear down, then deem that moment the
time I finally found home.
I never thought I was one to roam,
I would claim myself a 'homebody'
,but how is that even possible when I've never felt home
in this body? A rattling bag of bones, fat and flesh that have
done nothing but attack me my whole life.

So I think about leaving my body sometimes.
 I think about leaving it all,
　All of the time.

forgive me if I'm quiet
if I do not meet your standards of love
and support
I'm running on empty at the moment
and I cannot afford the gasoline.

It's not all butterflies and rainbows in a mind like mine

a steel blade reaches In and with one slice
takes the lashing from my tongue.
 I stare at it.
 on the ground. a bloodied little thing. pointless without

the acrid thoughts it would feed upon. yet they remain.

a vacuum of loathsomeness,
 a hunger for what?
 a poison apple placed in the palms of the ones I love.
 to what gain?
 a balm of shame coats the flesh and I am left-

I am left, I am left.

"you are so cold"

She's not my world
she's a world beside my own

Six degrees

the cool caress
of September's breath
held me this morn'
as I reached into
 gossamer lungs to
 find my own

a shudder crawled itself
under blankets of skin
braiding majesty into my bones

I was summoned to life
moulded by the fingers
of my flourishing

((whispers of a freshening
 borne of bygone sorrow

today,
I rise under the guise of Autumn
 under eyes half closed
perched upon the corners
 of a smile unpretended9
formed in the belly of a Summer
truly lived
truly loved
truly felt

you have called me complex before
you're not the first
not of this world
the fifth planet in possibility, love,
and stature
you are the first to simplify my being
you don't take credit for that
I call you humble, you call me silly
we get things backwards and talk to ourselves
we laugh it all off
I'll say it again and again until you get it
no one has ever loved me like you
I feel like I've been seen before,
but I was only Loved in bits and pieces
I wake up every morning knowing your Love in whole

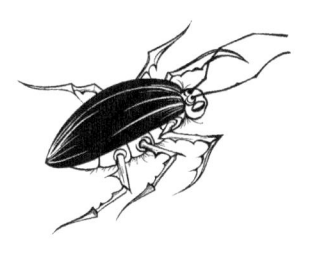

I can't think about it too much
I'll waste the whole day
making love to you in my head

' not everything is about you '

The wolf and the weeping willow

Could I sleep beneath you?
take the shade, and any moonbeam
that leaks through your sieve of branches.
could i lap like condensation
at your string light canopy and,
If you were to cry again,
could i lick the midnight from your face?
if i howled,
Would the wind make you moan?
should i ever roam,
would you always know that you are my home?

Collapsed

I say I can't fill my lungs with the breath that I need;
time stands still counting my heart beats.
An obsession? A fear of what?
Death.
It haunts me-
as I am taunted into the most violent of submissions.

I say I can't fill my lungs,
yet still I breathe.

Hellfire never felt so good

There is something about dusk.
especially on a summers eve'
night crawlers and creatures with wings pirouette
with grace. (some not so much)
and In these inferno skies they become more alive.
I write my name in figure eights in the sun dusted
screens and windows.
a memory, (if only temporary)
of a time I landed , upon a beautiful evening,
under now ominous hellfire skies.

I give up

*"i am not arguing with you,
i'm holding you accountable"*

snow falls from beyond the glass
I hold your hand, it's all I have

      the sky is...
         the trees are...
            the ground is...
               the walls are...
                  the floor is...
                     the sheets are...
                        white.

a mind is a cliff face
aging, soft deterioration
it is a diversion you don't stop staring at

like moonlight as a force of healing
like the crushing realization that love exists
in our greatest ache
that love exists at all
anything to keep us less than awake
for instance, I sleep on the sofa
to avoid missing bodies in my bed
this emptiness was what I feared the most
the feeling of need for another, the safety to be
or was it the fear that I am a loved vastness?

but thoughts, they creep in
tentacles tickle at my dopamine and it feels good
to see a way out, open a door and there it is …..
the escape from the darkness, the sunshine, the way out.

Temptations' vibrations run its course through
my battered veins and I rattle myself deeper into
the darkness adding extra chains to the bed.

 it's a day
 it's just the meds
 It's just a day

"i think we may have rushed into this"

My hands

my hands. have been the first hand to hold for
four new babies born of my own hand holding.
((in one shape or form))

my hands. have stolen pound coins from
my own mothers purse so i could buy cigarettes from the kids
at the smoking wall at school. shame attempts to claw itself
from. Memory. to lungs.
from lungs.... to my throat.

my hands took meals from my siblings.
to feed me supper ((food was uninvited))

my hands can count ten fingers, my mind adds three more. ((
these are times i never gave permission for them to be held,))
softly softly, softly, so softly so rr y.
((ten plus three times i let those fingers go))

my hand ((the right one)) tried to drain my blood from
the pretty part of the wrist
((the right one)) saved by someone else's hands

my hands prayed to no one,
my hands prayed to empty rooms in single beds
my hands prayed for safety
my hands prayed there was something more.

my hands. have been the first hand to hold for four new
babies born of my own hand holding. my hands and theirs

Church of us

Pure love, the original form of such
The love that is laced in all things living and nonliving
I cradle your heart in my hands
close them palm to palm in prayer

For even the gods sigh at our love, for all
That we are is good.

Can we kneel at our own feet?
Momentary revelations
Self redemption read out loud

Could we clasp hands, you and I?
In the Church of us
A house of mirrors
A house of trust

Show me church

Show me a place of worship no further from
here with me.

Refract rainbows from the stain glass
windows of our hearts

Baptise us with a spiritual cleansing of
permanent tomorrow's.

Liquid sunlight paints the ancient stone floor.
Steeping beds of moss that have pushed through
the foundations into a tea of reverence.

I ambrough there.
Pulled
Pushed

Whatever you may say.
I am gravitating towards this cushion of faith

Show me faith in love itself

If I call, will you answer?

Step Through the human boundaries and hold
me in our sacred space

Pull into stars from the abyss and use them as
stepping stones
to save me?

It saved me
We saved us

Through the misted eyes of the blind,
On bent knees you leaned in and lovingly
handed back my sight.

They made idols of one another

in seven sleeps I will reach skyward
run my fingers through the clear blue
along the mellow edges of the foothills
I will grab at handfuls of mountain run-off
cup the water in my palms
become an animal; primal creation
drag my lower lip across the sunset
press its peach skin against my tongue
fill my mouth with a river of surrender
eye every detail. each cascade. every pillar.
retrace my love across existence
write my name in figure eights
on trees. in the sand. against her stomach.
fall to my knees, weeping. smiling. pleasing.
pulling you in. on. over my soul.
my Body. my Mind. my Beloved.

time will stop, the stars will stare in awe
I'll bathe you in the moon
wrap you in golden rope and rosewater
I'll keep it between us
the way he looks at You.
you know.
You. Know.
they'll see it in my eyes. my poetry. my life.
that fire. your sight.
the way it changes and remains my home.
what I pray to. fall for. over and over.
You.

The trees are about to show us how beautiful it is to let go…

and let go they shall,
of precious memories held in the fists
of bygone sunny days.
 just as I let go of a tender grief held in the
palms of a summer lost to trouble and pain.

their beauty will fall into a
 tumble of sacrifice and rot
this rot will bloom surly from
 beneath a breast of breath

they will not cower from the elements,
 bare boned in defiance.
Instead they will sing in
harmony with the wind.

and though the bones may have broken,
and flesh most certainly bruised,

the trees are going to show that
of bark, of bone, of fern and of flesh
even in our death
we are beautiful when we let go

The things I miss, I cannot put into words.
they are feelings, experiences, moments,
only captured in a space where time fell
from its face, as we were held in its arms.
a living Polaroid never exposed,
just me and you in beautiful sepia tones.

Chronic pain

Just this once
I would like to open my
 eyes in the morning
free of worry
free of the hum and buzz
of this chronic pain
that haunts my bones
Invisible to all but me
just this once
I'd like to wake
and be completely free

It has all become beautifully rambunctious

dawn paints the night holding on stubbornly
to a sickled moon.

The skeletal remains of the old great Oak are changing,
 Its bones have now become homes for new life.

the horizons nakedness is heaving as if it's about
to break out in song, I swallow down the urge to
follow its lead.

She's breaking herself open, as a mother does.
and we are all awake to see her generosity celebrated,
In song,
In life,
I blooms,
In light.

We are all awake to see.

So please i ask In whispered tones, and gritted teeth politely,
 hold me with desire, in my desire to unapologetically
 break myself in half to set myself free.

today,
I rise under the guise of Autumn
under eyes half closed
perched upon the corners
of a smile unpretended9
formed in the belly of a Summer
truly lived
truly loved
truly felt

Equinox and the Horse chesnut tree

soles of feet, much smaller than my own shuffle
the sound of our journeys have changed.
 (decay hums Septembers song under a playful boot)
an earthworms feast has lain itself along their
pavement tables and forest floors.
What a feast. What a feast.

spiked jackets split themselves open revealing autumns
Jewels in beds of milky-white
silken beds.

The winds shake the trees filling little palms with fruits
of summer.
later filling buckets and sacks,then eventually our
home.

 memories flood back to the same rituals played with
my brothers, sister, Mother and Father
filling out pockets with gifts of the season.

I now chuckle as piles turn to mountains and
mountains to seas.

nowing that come winter i will be finding them
scattered around our home,
as my mum would back, all those years ago.

SO i feel i must express gratitude

I send thanks to the trees,
I praise love for the wind
I cheer thank you for equinox for thfe life time reminders,
 the summoning of memories,
 and for smiles on little faces,

I held you like it was the last time
it nearly was for any of us
swinging slowly,
life and time stood still
I shed a tear
it looked like a diamond on your shoulder
coincidence is far too coincidental sometimes
I'm holding you like it's the last time everytime
because love is this cold and broken moment
just like that one song sings

I'm nothing but a commodity to the people I love

you are static in a stormcloud
natural magnetism
I'm copper held to the highest point
I feel you
a pending thunderclap
running along the wet night sky
cracking at the Earth in a surging flash
a rumble in the distance rolling closer still
I'm at the curb, mouth open to the rain
aching for your current to reach my ground
again

Add a heading

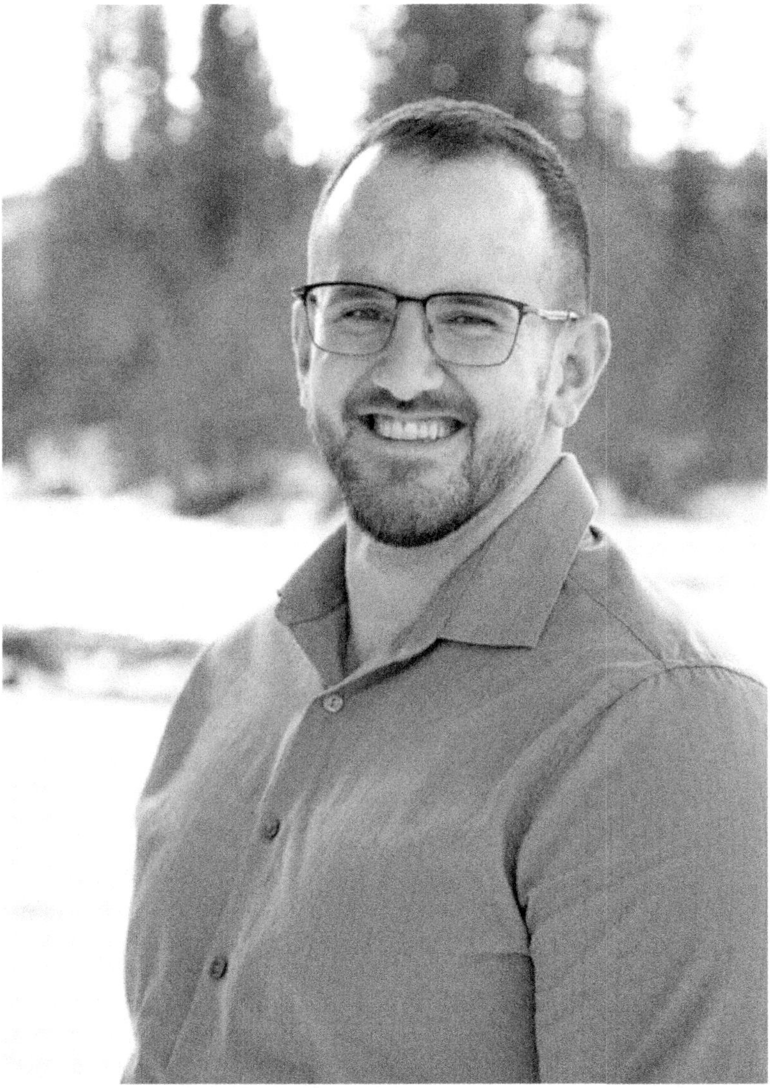

Erik Langford is a Canadian word feeler from Edmonton, Alberta. Growing up with a large family and a traumatic childhood, he fell into unhealthy coping mechanisms as a teenager and young adult until he discovered writing and poetry at the age of twenty eight. He aims to use this art to address his own truth in feeling on society, relationships, and the self in both positive and negative aspects with faith that it can help another to address their own surely peculiar existence, and it's relation to this mad and beautiful world. A believer of everything and nothing, Erik loves to explore different approaches to the spiritual and magickal parts of his life, and observe how so many different conclusions can make himself and others better for using these beliefs.

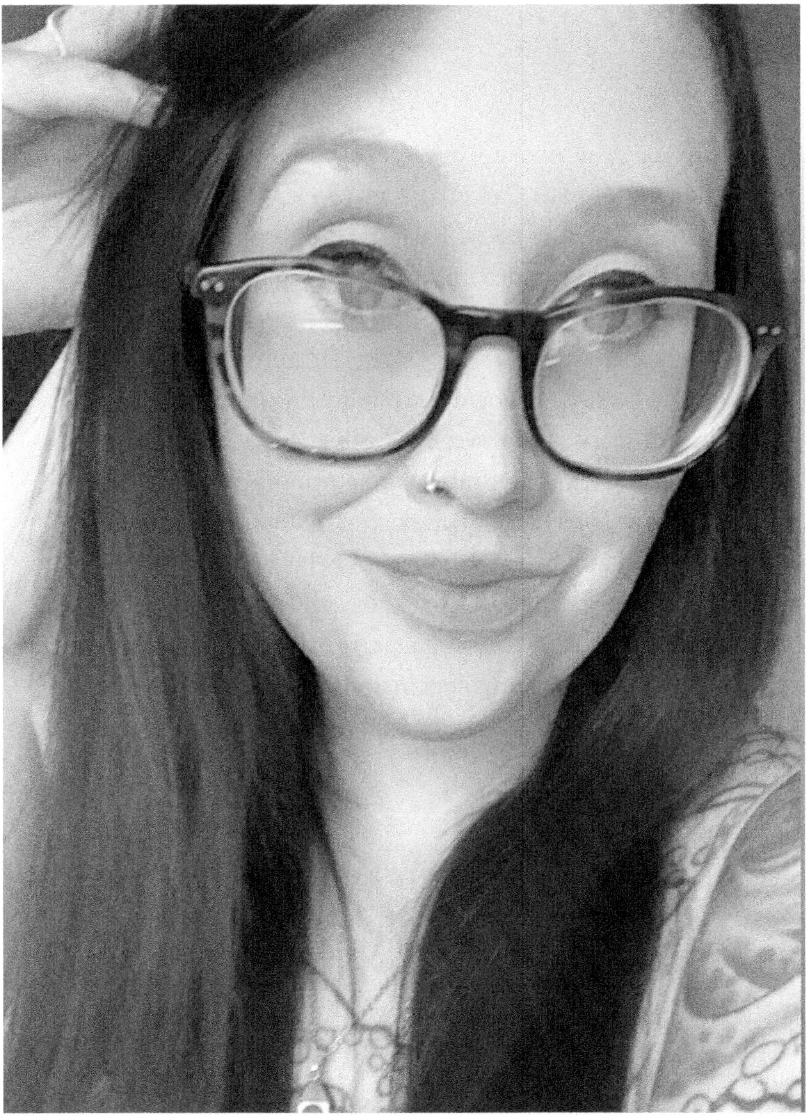

Hey my name is Emily. I Started to write as a way to escape from the world (and myself), empty my mind of all the goodness it carries and to share my love and passion for words and all they have given me.

I started reading when I was about six and writing for as long as I can remember. Some of the stories I love most are tales of magic and fantastical places I have gotten lost in, time and time again. Jennifer Armentrout, Terry Pratchett, Tolkinen, Neil Gaiman and C.S Lewis are just a few of the authors who have given me new worlds to call my own.

I love anything that's a little odd and magical, and found that in my writing, I feel most comfortable when I draw on nature and the deep wonder of this beautiful place we call home. I started out journaling and grew into poetry, which I started sharing a few years ago. I often look to my favorite poets for inspiration - Mary Oliver, Pablo Neruda, Alejandra Pizarnik, Paz.

I lush ya really

Add a subheading

Printed in Great Britain
by Amazon